香港國際詩歌之夜 *2015*
INTERNATIONAL POETRY NIGHTS IN HONG KONG

編輯 Editors

北島 Bei Dao

陳嘉恩 Shelby K. Y. Chan

方梓勳 Gilbert C. F. Fong

柯夏智 Lucas Klein

馬德松 Christopher Mattison

宋子江 Chris Song

目錄 Contents

水田宗子
Noriko Mizuta

深い眠りがあったら

深い眠りがあったら
目覚めてくるものがあろうに
季節が移れば
野の草も蕾を付けてくるように

列車に乗っているならば
後ろにおいていくものものに
別れの一瞥をなげかければいい
河の土手に立ちすくんでいた男
踏切で手をつないでいた幼い兄弟

すべては一瞬の決別
後ろに過ぎ去って行くスピードは
わたしの脚では
取り戻しに走れない

微睡んでいるのは
深い円筒の中
まわりながら
滑りながら

どこまで行っても不十分な

落下

底なしの誘惑

奈落まで落ちる覚悟でも

辿り着けない

傷口へ

目覚めが頼りの

願望

微睡んでいるのは谺の中

無すら反復する深い幻の谷間

霧の中から

還り続ける

音無しの音

過ぎ去らぬ時のエコー

如若沉睡

如若沉睡
總有甚麼會來喚醒
正如時光荏苒
野草也會長出花蕾

如若搭乘列車
向車尾消逝的一切
投上離別的一瞥便已足夠
河堤上呆立不動的男子
道口上牽著手年幼的兄弟

一切都是一瞬間的訣別
向後退去的速度
我的雙腳
無法追回

假寐
是在深深的圓筒中
繞啊繞
滑啊滑

到哪裏都不滿意
墜落
無底的誘惑
連一落到底的覺悟都
無法到達
向傷口
許下清醒藉以仰仗的
願望
假寐是在回聲中
連「無」都會反覆的幻覺之深谷
從霧裏
不斷回歸的
無聲之聲
——無法成為過去的時間回聲

(田原、毛乙馨　譯)

If You Happen into a Deep Sleep

If you happen into a deep sleep,
An awakening will certainly follow,
Just as when the seasons change
And the field grasses put forth new buds

If you're riding on a train,
It's fine to send parting glances back
Toward all the things you leave behind
A man standing transfixed on a river embankment
Young siblings holding hands at a railway crossing

Everything is a momentary farewell
The speed of things disappearing behind,
I cannot reverse
Cannot run back to regain

Drifting off to sleep,
In a deep cylinder
Spinning away
Slipping away

Not enough, no matter how far it goes

Dropping

Bottomless temptation

Resolved to fall even to the underworld,

Never arriving

At the wound

Awakening's reliable

Aspiration

What is drifting to sleep amidst echoes

Reverberating nothing through the deep phantom
valley

Out of the mist

Making its way home

Soundless sound

Never departing, echo of time

(Translated by Jordan A. Yamaji Smith)

詩は待っていてくれると

詩は待っていてくれると
T・S・エリオットは言った
魂は待っていてくれるだろうか
藪の中に潜んで
あるいは草原で寝転んで
わたしが追いつくのを
それとも
不意打ちをしてくれるだろうか
どこかで待ち伏せをして
辻斬りの腕でも試そうと

わたしも待っているのだろうか
こうして街を歩いていれば
あてどない放浪に似た
通過するばかりの
詩の中で
偶然出会うのではないか
向こうからこともなげに近づいてくる
見知らぬ国を通り過ぎていけば
突然背後から

呼び止められる
観光に訪れた
太古の廃墟で
地べたに座り込んでいるのではないか

わたしは見つめ続けてきた
爆発でできた宇宙が
ブラックホールに吸い込まれて
やがてすっかり消えてしまうように
わたしが記憶していた日々が
地の一点に吸い込まれていくのではと
それを見届けようと
この庭に舞い上がる
木の葉や灰塵に預けられた
魂のようなものが
徐々に
飛び散っていくのを

どこまで追っても
その先まで行き着けない

行く先定まらぬ旅路の物語を
どこかで語る詩人が現れるのを
詩はほんとうに
待っていてくれるのだろうか

如果詩會等待

T. S. 艾略特說過
如果詩會等待
那麼，靈魂也會等我吧
藏於草叢
或臥躺草原
抑或
突然襲擊
我的苦苦追尋
總之它潛伏在某處
等待著嘗試武士手腕的初斬

我好像也在等待吧
如果這樣走在街上
猶如毫無目的地流浪
在剛剛經過的
詩歌中
難道不是偶然遇見了嗎？
從對面滿不在乎地靠近
如果穿越未知的國度
突然從背後

被人叫住
在旅行到訪過的
太古的廢墟上
難道不是正席地而坐嗎？

我不停地凝視
因爆炸而形成的宇宙
被黑洞吸入
很快消失殆盡
我記憶中的日子
也會被大地上的某一點吸走
為見證這一切
它們飄揚在這個庭院
被託付給樹葉和灰塵
靈魂般的東西
慢慢地
飛散開去

無論追到哪裏
也無法抵達終點

在某地講述去處不明、旅途物語的
詩人現身之前
詩歌真的
會等待嗎？

（田原、毛乙馨　譯）

Poetry Will Wait for Me

Poetry will wait for me
T. S. Elliot wrote
I wonder if my soul will wait as well—
Lurking in the underbrush
Or sprawled on the field—
For me to come following
Or else
To greet me with surprise attack
Laying an ambush somewhere
Planning to test its new blade on my neck

Will I be waiting too?
Walking through town like this
Aimlessly, like a vagabond
In poetry
That just passes through,
Will we not end up meeting?
Careless approaching from over there
As I pass through this unknown country,
Leaping suddenly from the background

To challenge me
In these ancient ruins
Where I've come to sightsee
Here it is, sitting flat on bare earth

I have been staring at
This universe composed of explosion
As though inhaled by a black hole
Finally, disappearing,
These days I've held as memories
Inhaled into a single spot on the earth
Something like my spirit
Oversees as though to assure
That the leaves, ashes and dirt
Whirling up in this custodial garden
Gradually
Are scattered away

No matter how far it pursues
It can never arrive at the end

Where somewhere a poet will appear to tell
Tales from a road with unfixed destination
Will poetry really
Wait for that, I wonder?

(Translated by Jordan A. Yamaji Smith)

化石博物館にて

長い暗闇の中を上って来た
ゆっくりと時間をかけて
思えば
時間などあったのか
長いか短いか
自分だけ
といって
自分がわかってきたわけではない
樹か
石か
上へ上へ
少しずつ
頑なに
周りには
柔らかくなっていくものもの
下へ下へと
着実に
時を刻んでいる
気配
形を崩し
落ちてくるものを受け入れ

ああ　何というこの固さ
生き延びる
この冷たさ
吸収されない

ここに在り続ける
自分のまま
一〇〇億年
二〇〇億年
動かなかった
消えようともしなかった
溶けない軀
さようなら
暖かい湿り気
さようなら
醒めない眠り
遠いと近い
小さいと大きい
自分のまま
解けない意志

風の中で揺れた
光と雨をもとめて
手足を
のばせるだけのばした
夢の中の
意識の残影
周りに花々は咲いていたか
石のように
黙り
巨木のように
天を仰ぎ
一番乗りの孤独
その時
その小さい身体で
永遠を夢見
心を閉ざしたのか

気がつくと
見られている
ガラスの中の固いヒーロー

初めて花咲いた
晒しもの
意固地に生き残ろうと
石になった
あの美しさで
あの若さで
メドゥサに睨まれた
滅びゆく美から
朽ちない固さへ
そして
晒される栄光へ
電光のガラスケースの
灼熱のスポットライト
初犯の永久戦犯
最初に見つけられた功績
ガラスの中の永遠
それでも一〇〇億年がせいぜいの
瞬間の出来事
大きな建物の中の
一幕ものの舞台劇
初めて咲いた花の

ストーリー不明の物語
学者もわからぬ
シナリオライターはどこだ
遅れてやって来た
演出家
色のない
形だけ
身振りも台詞もない
寸劇の
なんという機嫌の良さ
なんという明るい舞台
なにもかも
封じ込めた
この感動

在化石博物館

從漫長的黑暗中爬出
花時間慢慢
思考
時間真的存在過嗎？
是長還是短？
雖說
孑然一身
卻並不了解自己
是樹木？
是石頭？
向上、向上
一點一點地
變得頑固
周圍全是
變軟之物
向下、向下
踏實地
雕刻時光
跡象的
形狀崩潰
接納墜落之物

啊啊，這是何等的堅硬
這個倖存下來的
冰涼
不被吸收

廝守於此
按著自己的樣子
一百億年
兩百億年
一動不動
甚至從不打算消失
不溶化的軀體
再見
溫潤的濕氣
再見
不醒的沉睡
遠和近
小和大
按著自己的樣子
從不鬆懈的意志

搖曳於風中

希求光和雨

極盡所能

伸展四肢

夢中的

意識之殘影

花朵在四周綻放了嗎？

石頭一樣

沉默

如參天大樹

仰望天空

最先抵達的孤獨

那時

用它小小的身體

夢見永遠

有過壓抑嗎？

緩過神來

被觀賞的

玻璃裏堅硬的英雄

第一次開了花

曾被唾棄

卻堅挺地存活下來

變成石頭

以那種美

和那種鮮活

與美杜莎對視

從走向滅亡的美

向著不朽的堅硬

而後

暴露於榮光之中

電光的玻璃罩裏

灼熱的聚光燈

初犯的永久戰犯

最初被發現的功績

玻璃罩裏的永遠

儘管如此，百億年也不過

只是彈指一揮間

是雄偉建築物裏

舞臺劇的一幕

初次綻放的花朵的
不明情節的故事
學者也不明白
編劇在哪兒
遲來的
演出家
無色
僅有形狀
沒有動作和臺詞
短劇
是多麼的快活
舞臺又是多麼的明亮
一切都能
包容
此刻的感動

（田原、毛乙馨　譯）

On the Fossil Museum

Rising through the long darkness
Slowly, taking its time
I reflect
Was there such thing as time?
So long, so brief
By myself
This
Isn't something I could come to understand
A tree?
A rock?
Upward, upward
Gradually
Obstinately
Through its surroundings
Substance that grows soft
Downward, downward
Steadily
Engraving time
Signs
Destroying shapes
Taking in things that come falling

Ah,   how to describe this hardness
Long-living
This chill
That cannot be absorbed

Remaining here
Just as it is
Ten billion years
Twenty billion years
It did not move
Or disappear
Unmelting body
Goodbye
Warm moisture
Goodbye
Unwakening sleep
Far and near
Small and large
Just as it is
Unbreakable volition

It shook in the wind
Seeking sunshine and rain
Extended its limbs
As far as it could
Remnants of consciousness
In a dream
Did flowers bloom all around?
Like a rock
Staying silent
Like a giant tree
Revering the heavens
Leading the charge into solitude
That time
That small body
Did your heart close
Dreaming of forever?

Suddenly realizing,
It's being watched
Hero in hard glass

In first bloom
Bleached cotton
Obstinately trying to survive,
It became rock
With such beauty
Such youth,
Under Medusa's glare
From perishable beauty
To undecaying solidity
And
To refined glory
Lighted glass case
Incandescent stoplight
First offense of an immortal war criminal
First achievements discovered
Eternity in glass
Though at most, a ten-billion-year
Moment's worth of events
A one-act play performed
In a large building

First flowers to blossom
Epic of obscurity
Incomprehensible to scholars
Where are the screenwriters?
They've arrived so late
The directors
Colorless
Only with form
Without gestures or lines
This skit with
Such a fine mood
Such a bright stage
Anything, everything
Contained in
This action

(Translated by Jordan A. Yamaji Smith)

青の詩

記憶が薄れていく先は
青い空
野原に寝転んで行く先を追う
青が終わるところに昔があるのか
青が虚ろになるところは
白いナッシング
闇でないのがいい
空はすっぽりとあたりを包み
草原いっぱいの忘却
どこにも手がかりはない

わたしは
薄れた記憶を吸い込む
味のない
青

藍之詩

記憶褪色的前方
是藍天
橫躺在草原去追趕那前方
藍的盡頭難道還有往昔？
在藍成為空洞之際
只有白色的虛無
不是黑暗就已足夠
天空覆蓋周圍
草原充滿忘卻
不論哪裏都茫無頭緒

我
吸入褪色的記憶
和無味的
藍

(田原、毛乙馨　譯)

Poem in Blue

Where memory goes fading on
Blue sky
Tumbling to the field, I follow
Where the blue ends, could long-ago be there?
Where blue goes blank
A white nothing
Better yet, a not-darkness
Sky envelops everything around
A meadow's worth of oblivion
Nowhere so much as a trace

I
Inhale that faded memory
Flavorless
Blue

(Translated by Jordan A. Yamaji Smith)

庭師 ── 庭1

今朝も男は庭を掃いている
竹箒を手に
落ち葉をかき集め
土にかすかな爪痕を残し
この囲みとられた小さな土地を
丁寧に浄めている

今朝も男は庭を掃いている
昨日も木の葉は散った
この庭に植えられ
この庭に休むことなく葉を落とす
樹々とともに
男は時を掃いていく
一夜のうちに過ぎて行ったものもの
はらはらと落ち
いつの間にかかき集められ
浄められていく
ものもの
男の竹箒は休むことはない
見て見ぬ振りをし
無関心にやり過ごし

やがて仕返しをされるのは
不意打ちであってほしいと
願うわたしは
庭師が頼りだ
庭師の腕がすべてだ
証拠を消し去り
跡形もなく
始末する
わたしの庭の僧侶
不浄な時に対面し
後始末をし続ける
職人技
囲っても囲っても
忍び込んでくる蔦のように
いつの間にか
庭の暗闇で待ち伏せているものを
朝にはかき集め
かすかな掃き目で整え
一日
見通しのよい

陽のあたる場所にする
庭の守番

春も夏も葉は落ち続け
秋も冬も葉は蘇り続ける
庭師の季節に終わりはない
黒衣の庭師
今朝も庭を掃いている

園藝師——庭院 1

今天早晨，男人又在打掃庭院
手持竹掃帚
將落葉掃到一起
地上留下些許的帚痕
在被圈起的一小片土地上
細心地掃淨

今天早晨，男人又在打掃庭院
昨天樹葉也落下
長在這庭院裏的樹
無休止地飄下落葉
與樹木一起
男人打掃著時光
一夜間消失的東西
紛紛飄落
不知不覺被掃在一起
乾乾淨淨地
將它們掃盡
男人的竹掃帚從不停歇
我卻對他視而不見

甚至漠不關心
讓我不久遭到報應
最好以突然襲擊的方式
許下這個願望的我
園藝師才是依靠
園藝師的本領就是一切
銷毀證據
蹤跡全無
處理善後
我庭院中的僧侶
不潔時會出現
以匠人的絕技
繼續清理
無論怎樣圍起院子
都像悄悄潛入的攀緣莖
不知不覺地
在早晨，將埋伏庭院暗處的東西
掃到一起
留下些許帚痕
一整天

眼界開闊
朝陽之處
充當庭院的守衛者

春夏樹葉都不停飄落
秋冬樹葉又不斷復甦
園藝師的季節裏沒有終結
穿黑衣的園藝師
今天早晨又在打掃著庭院

(田原、毛乙馨　譯)

The Gardener—*Garden* 1

This morning too, he is sweeping the garden
Bamboo broom in hand
Raking up the fallen leaves
Leaving faint scratches in the dirt
This tiny, enclosed plot of earth
He so carefully purifies

This morning too, he is sweeping the garden
Yesterday the leaves fell once more
Planted in this garden
This garden never rests, constantly shedding leaves
Along with the trees
He goes on sweeping time
This-and-thats which have come to pass in a single night
Fluttering down
Gathered up in a blink
Purifying these
This-and-thats
His bamboo broom never resting
Pretending not to see

Unselfconsciously working away
I want his eventual revenge
To be a surprise attack,
Praying this,
I depend on the gardener
The gardener's skill is all
Sweeping away the evidence
No vestige left
He finishes
Priest of my garden,
Facing up to time's defilements,
Continues to tidy up
Craftsmanship
Try as he might to preserve it,
Stealing in like ivy
In a blink
In the morning, gathering up
These things that ambush him in the garden's darkness
He handles with subtle sweeps
In one day

Creating a place with clear views
Where the sun shines
The garden's protector

Come spring, come summer, the leaves go on falling
Come autumn, come winter, the leaves go on
   rejuvenating
No end to the gardener's season
The gardener, in black clothes,
This morning too, he is sweeping the garden

(Translated by Jordan A. Yamaji Smith)

紫陽花──庭6

梅雨前線に異常があって
紫陽花は青空の下で咲いている
照りつける日差しの中で
色を変える暇もなく
変身し遂げる余裕もなく
祭りをもりたてもしないで
一直線に満開

急がないで
急がないで
それでもあじさいは花
急いでも急がなくても
今年は終わり

紫陽花——庭院6

梅雨前線發生了異常
紫陽花在晴空下綻放
毒曬的日光裏
既無暇變色
也無力變身
更不為節日添色
一直盛開

不用急
不用急
即使如此，紫陽花依然是花
無論急還是不急
今年到此為止

(田原、毛乙馨　譯)

Hydrangeas—*Garden* 6

Rather odd for the season of early summer rains
Hydrangeas, blooming under blue sky
Under the all-illuminating sunshine
No time for their color to deepen,
Too rushed for a full transformation
Without quite livening up the festival,
They burst into full blossom

Don't hurry
Don't hurry
But hydrangeas are after all a flower
Whether they hurry or not
This year will end

(Translated by Jordan A. Yamaji Smith)

〈くちなし〉の巻 —— 佐川亜紀との四行連詩より

昨日は白かったのに　今日はもう土色

狡猾なくちなし

時の先回りをして

死をやり過ごそうとの変身術

*

メール送信にしっぱい

指と頭をつなぐ古びた回線のトラブル

しまい込んできたわたしの告白は

超特急で見知らぬひとへの落雷

梔子之卷——與佐川亞紀的四行連詩

昨天還是白的，今天卻成土黃
狡猾的梔子
搶在時間之前
是意圖逃避死亡的變身術
*
郵件發送失敗
連接手指和大腦的老式線路出了問題
保存起我的表白
是朝向陌生人的超特快落雷

（田原、毛乙馨　譯）

"Gardenias"—Verse from Four-line *Renshi* with Sagawa Aki

Though white yesterday   today, already the color of dirt
Sly gardenias
Forestalling time itself
Trying to bypass death with their transformative craft
*
The attempt to send the email failed
Some trouble in that aged circuit between fingertip
   and brain
My once deeply concealed confession
A lightning bolt Super-Expressed to unknown
   addressees

(Translated by Jordan A. Yamaji Smith)

〈ガラス〉の巻——木島始との四行連詩より

ボストンは自殺した詩人たちの街
だが　この六月の日
街は一枚のガラスのように光り
どこにも記憶はない
*
落書きのようにとりとめのない
あなたからのEメールのすべてを
6・8メガバイトの感度で保存する
いいかげんな心でメモリーはいっぱい
*
引越しのたびに燃やしてきたノートの束
旅に出ては忘れてきた他人のことば
舞いの彼方に消えていった蜉蝣の言の葉
ある日稲妻となって突然闇から還ってくる

玻璃之卷——與木島始的四行連詩

波士頓是詩人自殺的城市
然而，在這六月的一天
城市好似一塊發光的玻璃
哪裏都不存在記憶
*

像亂塗亂畫一樣天馬行空
你發送的電子郵件全部
以6.8百萬位元組的速度保存
馬馬虎虎的心裏全是記憶體
*

搬家時燒毀的一捆捆筆記
出門旅行時忘掉別人的語言
飛向遠方消失不見的蜉蝣之語
某一天變成閃電從黑暗中忽然出現

(田原、毛乙馨　譯)

"Glass"—Verse from Four-line *Renshi* with Kijima Hajime

Boston, city of poets' suicide
Yet   this June day
The city shines like a single glass
Memory is nowhere
*

Your emails like endlessly scrawling graffiti
I always save them
In 6.8 megabyte sensitivity
My heart's memory is full to brimming
*

Bundles of notebooks I've set ablaze whenever we
    moved
What set out on the journey were forgotten words
    from some other
Words of a mayfly dancing off to vanish over yonder
One day, transformed into lightning, they come
    zooming back from the darkness

(Translated by Jordan A. Yamaji Smith)

水田宗子，著名詩人和女性學批評家。水田宗子在東京女子大學文理學部畢業後，赴耶魯大學留學並取得美國文學博士學位。先後在美國多所大學任教，1985 年為創建城西短期大學回國，1992 年創立城西國際大學。著有詩集《歸路》、《聖塔芭芭拉的暑假》、《綠藻之海》等。評論集有《從女主人公到英雄——女性的自我與表現》、《20世紀的女性表現——朝向性差異的外部》、《語言紡織羽衣——女性的行旅物語》、《現代主義思潮與「戰後女性詩歌」的發展》、《大庭美奈子的記憶文學》以及英文專著《埃德加・愛倫・坡的世界——罪與夢》、《近代日本文學中的現實與虛構》等。水田宗子翻譯有多部童話集和女性批評專著。她曾獲得瑞典駐東京大使館主辦的馬丁松國際詩歌獎，也被匈牙利政府授予共和國文化勳章，並獲世界數十所大學頒授名譽博士和名譽教授，現為日本城西大學理事長。

Noriko Mizuta's free-verse poetry has blended trans-national feminist perspectives with meditations on the meaning of family and home through five decades. Mizuta joined the Boomerang Society poetry circle when she was an undergraduate in Japan. She then continued writing in the U.S., publishing *End of Spring* (1976) and *Interlude* (1980), and co-authored *Amber in Flames* (1996) with Ohba Minako, while living in Riverside, California. Mizuta returned to Japan in 1985, and published her major critical works of modern Japanese women writers. She has established together with Chinese poets the Japan-China Association for Short Poetry. Mizuta has also translated works by Sylvia Plath, Anne Sexton, and E. Ann Kaplan into Japanese. In 2009, she founded the poetry journal *Carillon Street*. Recent collections have included *The Road Home* (2008); the three-part *Summer Holidays in Santa Barbara* (2010), *A Wedding in Amsterdam* (2013), *Sabbath in Tokyo* (2015), and *Sea of Blue Algae* (2013), which explores themes of the life-cycle, humans' origins and destinations, and the acceptance of mourning. Mizuta received the Cikada Prize (2013), founded to commemorate Swedish poet and Nobel laureate, Harry Martinson.

出版 Publisher
香港中文大學出版社 The Chinese University Press

封面影像 Cover Image
北島 Bei Dao

出版日期 Date of Publication
二零一五年十一月 November 2015

國際書號 ISBN
978-962-996-728-4

香港國際詩歌之夜 2015 International Poetry Nights in Hong Kong 2015
主辦單位 Organizer
香港中文大學文學院 Faculty of Arts, The Chinese University of Hong Kong

協辦單位 Co-organizers
香港中文大學中國文化研究所
Institute of Chinese Studies, The Chinese University of Hong Kong
香港中文大學出版社 The Chinese University Press
香港兆基創意書院 HKICC Lee Shau Kee School of Creativity
廣州時刻文化傳播有限公司 Moment Communications

贊助 Sponsors
香港法國文化協會 Alliance Française de Hong Kong
上海廿一文化發展有限公司 Shanghai 21 Culture Promotion Co., Ltd.
中國會 The China Club
香港文學出版社有限公司 The Hong Kong Literary Press Co. Limited
斑馬谷文化發展（北京）有限公司 Zebra Valley Culture Development